The Naked I: Monologues from Beyond the Binary

A Play in Two Acts

Tobias K. Davis

The Naked I: Monologues from Beyond the Binary received its world premiere at Smith College in Northampton, MA in March of 2003, directed by Tobias K. Davis and Claire Avitabile (www.tctwentypercent.org).

Cover and Interior Layout by Sylvia Altreuter and Miriam Roberts.
Edited by Tobias K. Davis, Miriam Roberts and Sylvia Altreuter.

To all the brilliant, creative, bold, and honest trans*, intersex, and gender variant people who shared their stories with me. This work would not have been possible without you.

CONTENTS

ACKNOWLEDGMENTS

A huge thank you to the many people who made this work
possible:
To my partner cmoore who has seen this play almost as
many times as I have and still laughs at all the right places.
To Claire Avitabile who has been beside me literally and
figuratively for the entire life of this piece – you make
dreams come true again and again. Please direct everything
I ever write.
To Len Berkman for your edits, your laugh, and your title.
To Sylvia Altreuter, intrepid editor and designer.
And lastly, a huge thank you to the many many producers,
directors, actors, and crews who have brought this piece to
life in the past and to those who will in the future.

CAST OF CHARACTERS
(in order of appearance)

Three Gender "Freaks"
Interviewer
Subject
Trans Woman, 51 years old
FtM, 15 years old
Lauren, a Transgender Woman, 22 years old
Graeme, a Straight, Cisgender Man in his mid-30s
Esther, an Intersex Woman in her mid-40s
Lannie, a Transgender Woman
Daniel, a Transgender Man
3 Doctors
Lover
A Gender Freak
Another Gender Freak
A Fantasy Woman
Jim, a Young Boy
School Nurse
tyle, a Genderqueer
Anthony, a Transgender Man in his early-20s
A Cute Girl, in her early-20s
Jesse, a young Transgender Man

NOTES

Note on Authorship:
Many of these monologues were written in part, or entirely, by their contributors. I served as editor, adapting stories, poems, and survey responses for the stage. I have indicated the author/contributor under the title of each piece, including a few who wanted to remain anonymous. If there is no author named, it means I wrote that piece. Permissions have been obtained to use all names as written.

Note on Characters:
This piece is written for an ensemble of at least four actors. Ideally these would portray as wide a range of gender diversity as the monologues themselves do. It is not necessary for the actor to share the same gender identity as the character (in fact, it can be provocative if they do not), but please respect the identities of the characters at all times.

Each actor may play many characters of varying ages and identities, or you are welcome to use a large cast with a different actor for each character.

Some characters appear in more than one piece, but it is not necessary to use the same actor for each.

Note on Language:
Sometimes in stage directions for gender-ambiguous or genderqueer characters I use the third-gender pronouns "ze" (for he/she) and "hir" (for his/her). It seemed more appropriate not to give a binary gender pronoun to a non-binary character.

Note on Stage Directions:
This script contains some of the stage directions of the world premiere of the play at Smith College, March 7-9 2003. However, future directors are encouraged to ignore the directions completely and do their own thing!

ACT ONE

INTRODUCTION

THREE GENDER "FREAKS"

Lights up on FREAK 1 sitting on the table. As they speak, FREAK 2 and FREAK 3 pop out from behind the table. They whirl around, striking poses as they speak.

FREAK 1:	Are you still worried?
FREAK 2:	We are.
FREAK 3:	We're still worried about genitals.
FREAK 1:	Like in the *Vagina Monologues*?
FREAK 2:	Exactly. Eve Ensler started the conversation in that play when she opened the Vagina's mouth.
FREAK 3:	Thanks, Eve!
FREAK 2:	But we're still worried. Because once she let those silenced vaginas talk, a whole lot of other genitals wanted to take the stage too.
FREAK 3:	So that's what we're here for. To keep talking.
FREAK 1:	And we've got a lot of voices.
FREAK 2:	Transgender voices.
FREAK 3:	Intersex voices.
FREAK 1:	Queer voices.

FREAK 2: And countless others. A whole lot of genitals out there don't fit too well into male or female. I mean, what do you call a man with a vagina? Or a woman with a penis? Or a person with both, neither, or something altogether different?

FREAK 3: *(Interrupting.)* And equally exciting.

FREAK 2: If it was made by a doctor when you were two days old, is it still a vagina? If it used to be the skin on the inside of your arm, can you truly call it a penis?

FREAK 1: Sure you can.

FREAK 3: Or not.

FREAK 2: That's what we're here to discuss.

FREAK 1: *(Placing arms around the other FREAKS.)* Cunts and cocks and dildos and asses and more! We got genitals so cool they haven't even named us yet!

FREAK 3: So instead, we made up our own names.

FREAK 1: Boydick

FREAK 2: Man pussy

FREAK 1: Clit on a Stick

FREAK 2: Almostcunt

FREAK 3: Junk

FREAK 1: Boyjunk

FREAK 3:	Wang
FREAK 1:	Biz
FREAK 2:	The bitch
FREAK 1:	Knob
FREAK 2:	The Werewolf's Maw
FREAK 3:	The puss
FREAK 2:	Rubber Hose
FREAK 1:	My hose
FREAK 3:	Magic Wand
FREAK 2:	Magic Dick
FREAK 1:	Tootsie Roll
FREAK 3:	Big Clit
FREAK 1:	Dicklet
FREAK 2:	Cocklet
FREAK 3:	Minicock
FREAK 1:	Hot Button
FREAK 2:	Temp Cunt
FREAK 1:	Cock Mask
FREAK 3:	Detachable Penis
FREAK 2:	Inside-Out Cunt

FREAK 1:	Inside-Out Cock
FREAK 3:	Extra Tranny Hole
FREAK 2:	Fisting Hole
FREAK 1:	Earth Hole
FREAK 2:	Front Hole
FREAK 1:	Glory Hole
FREAK 3:	Auxiliary Asshole
FREAK 1:	Guy Pie
FREAK 3:	The Decoration
FREAK 2:	Bonus Round
FREAK 3:	Down there
FREAK 1:	That Thing
FREAK 2:	Nasty Thing
FREAK 3:	Nothing.

NOTHING

INTERVIEWER, SUBJECT

The SUBJECT should look increasingly more uncomfortable and mortified. Part of hir wants to respond, of course, but ze can't bring hirself to answer any of the questions. Neither of these are realistic people, rather representations. The INTERVIEWER speaks in a robotic monotone, like a recorded voice, smiling in a mechanical imitation of friendliness (ze may even be replaced by a recorded voice). The SUBJECT is as emotional as the INTERVIEWER is unemotional.

INTERVIEWER: Please, come in, sit down, make yourself comfortable. Can I get you anything to drink? Coffee, tea?

(SUBJECT remains standing, looking lost.)

SUBJECT: *(Softly.)* No thanks.

INTERVIEWER: OK, then let's begin. First off, what led you to respond to this survey?

SUBJECT: I wanted to offer my atypical opinion; I don't see my experiences represented very often.

INTERVIEWER: Please give me as much identification as you feel comfortable with. For example: age, race, sexual orientation, gender identity, religion, "assigned" sex at birth and now, ethnic background, profession, where you are from, and where you live now.

SUBJECT: OK. I am ageless, you'll find me in any country, in any era, all over the planet. I

am homosexual, heterosexual, bisexual,
pansexual, asexual, queer, questioning,
and confused. I'm male, female, intersex,
transgender and cisgender. I am Pagan,
Christian, Jewish, Muslim, Atheist,
Agnostic, Hindu, Buddhist and more. I'm
working-class, middle-class, upper-class.
I'm on Wall Street, and in the poorest
village of Africa. I'm a computer
programmer and a factory worker. I'm
struggling to live, I'm living it up, I'm dead
in the streets. No one knows if it was
murder or suicide. *(Pause.)* I am nobody,
I am nothing, and I am everybody and
everything.

INTERVIEWER: Tell me about your genitals.

*(No response, the next question is to guide the SUBJECT.
On each negative response, the Interviewer tries the next
question to stimulate more of a reaction.)*

INTERVIEWER: What do your genitals look like?

SUBJECT: I never look.

INTERVIEWER: Have you always had the same physical
genitalia?

SUBJECT: I'd prefer not to talk about that.

INTERVIEWER: What do you call your genitals? What did
you call your genitals as a child? What do
your lovers call your genitals?

SUBJECT: Nothing. Ever.

INTERVIEWER: How do your genitals feel?

SUBJECT: I don't want to talk about it.

INTERVIEWER: What do your genitals do?

SUBJECT: Nothing good!

INTERVIEWER: What do you or other people do with them?

SUBJECT: That's a really personal question, you know.

INTERVIEWER: Would you ever want to change your genitals? How? Would the change be permanent?

SUBJECT: *(Each response is definitive, yet differs completely in tone from the previous.)* Yes. *(Pause.)* No. *(Pause.)* Maybe.

INTERVIEWER: Has anything ever happened to your genitals that you didn't want?

SUBJECT: *(Loaded silence.)*

INTERVIEWER: *(As though ze has responded.)* Tell me about sex.

SUBJECT: *(Forcefully.)* No way.

INTERVIEWER: How do you feel about your genitals during sexual activities?

SUBJECT: I don't think in those terms...it's a part of my body. I consider my body somewhat treacherous....

INTERVIEWER: Relate any sexual experiences you feel illustrate your relationship to your genitals.

SUBJECT: My best sexual experiences allow me to transcend my body.

INTERVIEWER: Tell me about masturbation.

SUBJECT: *(Accusatory tone.)* You tell me. I haven't heard you offer any information here today.

INTERVIEWER: Tell me anything else.

SUBJECT: I think I'm finished here. I have nothing to say to you.

(SUBJECT exits. BLACKOUT on INTERVIEWER, still smiling obliviously.)

A TRANS WOMAN'S VAGINA MONOLOGUE
By Anonymous

TRANS WOMAN, 51 YEARS OLD

Lights up on TRANS WOMAN center stage, in front of the table. Theatrical pose, very aware of the audience.

Yeah, I've seen the Vagina Monologues, and it's my turn now:

A TRANS WOMANS VAGINA MONOLOGUE.

This is for V-day, and all the transgender people who have been violently abused.

This is for my own childhood that never was due to incest.

(Offstage voice asks.) If your vagina got dressed, what would it wear?

My vagina would wear a sun hat, yes a sun hat, I want my vagina to be out in the sun, basking in all its glory!

(Offstage voice asks.) If your vagina could talk, what would it say, in two words?

THANK YOU.

(To audience.) Yes my vagina would say thank you if it could talk; it would say thank you for the penile inversion surgery. Most people think about genital surgery as 'getting your penis cut off.' Losing your penis. But I have not lost anything. I have gained a vagina.

On February 25th, 2001 I awoke in the hospital. It was my 51st birthday, and my first day with a vagina. On Feb. 24th I had had a form of sexual reassignment surgery that constructed a vagina, right between my legs, where it should have been all my life.

(Sits up, facing the audience. Parts legs and examines herself under the gown.)

Yes! I have a vagina. Here I am a fifty-one-year-old woman with a one-day-old vagina. A puffy, sore vagina but it's mine. My vagina!

The doctor informed me that all had gone well, and that I was well packed to prevent it from closing up. I was still bleeding and in a lot of pain.

Still, I could die in peace now. My body, soul, brain, and spirit were whole at last. A court order declaring that I was a female was in the works!

Four days later, the packing came out of my vagina. Today was the day I would see my vagina for the first time. I could not hold back my tears as the nurse handed me a mirror.

I placed it between my legs and sat up to look.

(Sits up, turns to face the audience. Spreads legs, leans back to find that awkward angle necessary to view her vagina.)

I stared in amazement. My vagina was puffy and ugly! It was strange-looking. *(Reflects.)* Then again, I never saw a vagina from this angle before.

My vagina, yes my vagina, oozed out blood and other fluids for the next few months. At the age of 51 some women stop needing pads. But I was wearing them for the first time.

I also had to start dilating myself with a special device; the dilating procedure was an important part of my postoperative care.

(Stands, steps forward, takes off the robe.)

Six months later, and all the swelling has gone away, and the need to wear pads has gone down, and the bleeding has stopped.

(Walks back to the table — it is now a different place. Sits up with mirror as before.)

Once again I use the mirror to take a look at my vagina.

(Doesn't look yet.)

After all these years of self-loathing and feeling incomplete, I am afraid to look at my own vagina!

(Looks into mirror.)

My lips look too big!

(Stretches back to see everything.)

Still I hold them open with a mirror set up so I can see my vagina.

(Building excitement.)

I can see my vaginal orifice; I can see my urethral orifice and my clitoris.

(Sits back up, puts aside the mirror.)

I am crying again; you see, I have a vagina. I am a whole complete woman.

(Stands, walks toward audience.)

Dilating is no longer a medical chore, it now is joyful masturbation.

(Closes eyes, lets herself go.)

Feeling that vibrator deep inside me, finding that spot. That spot where if I hit it right, my whole body vibrates in delight. That spot is my vagina.

(Softly.) My vagina is me.

A YOUNG FTM'S DILEMMA
By AdriaN

FTM, 15 years old

Lights up on young FTM standing center stage. He wears baggy clothes and a baseball cap. His shoulders are hunched forward to hide his chest better, hands stuffed into his pockets. His voice is surly at first, but he warms to us as he goes on.

People associate vaginas with "she." I'm sure as Hell not a "she."

I have one, I know I have one. *(Pause.)* It never really felt like mine, though. It's like a little animal, you know, hairy...alien. Its current purpose is to torture me. It keeps me from doing stuff when it bleeds. It's hard to think of yourself as a guy when you're bleeding from the pussy. It keeps me from peeing standing up easily, *(Pause, proudly.)* though I do try — I'm a natural.

It has defined me as a female to society since birth.

On the forms, where they ask your sex, if they don't specify sex over gender, I check male, but my mom always corrects it. They ask, on the charts, "If female, when was your last period?" It pisses me off. I'm male, and I have periods. I'm male, in a female body. I was marked down as female, told I was female, forced to grow up female. I was confused, I denied it, and then realized: I'm male.

But the world sees me as the gender I'm not, because of what I have between my legs.

I try to show them. I bind my chest, wear stereotypically male clothing (though since I'm 5' 1" I don't always pass that good), short hair, I do as much as I can without outing myself to my dad. I pack sometimes. *(Absently touches crotch to show "packing.")* On my good days I pass as a guy or butch dyke, on most days, I get people staring at me playing the boy-or-girl game. On my bad days, I don't pass at all.

Before I'd really given much thought to it, my best friend said a couple of times I acted like a guy in drag.

(Sits up on table, knees apart, almost a caricature of the "teenage boy slouch.")

My movements are mostly male, now. Yesterday, this guy at the deli called me "buddy." It was awesome. But then these two women at Starbucks called me ma'am, and I got real self-conscious.

(Discouraged.) It's like they can see through my clothes.

(Stands, as before.)

When I was a kid, I didn't think about my genitals. I didn't have to think about them. I called it a penis when I didn't know better. Kinda shocked my parents a bit. I thought, why not? I was a guy.

I think at one point, I actually believed that at puberty, I'd have the right genitals. *(Dramatically and joyously.)* Look mom, my penis grew in the night! But then my period came, and I hated my genitals. Still do.

(Confiding tone — embarrassed and hesitant.)

At one point I wondered whether I was born without a *(he can hardly get the word out)* clit, when I started thinking about sex reassignment surgery and how you needed one to change...and I had to find a way to ask my mom if I was born "missing anything" without her guessing what I was asking about. *(Defensive.)* How was I supposed to know what it looked like? I'm a virgin! *(Beat.)* Oh, and I do have one, by the way.

Now, I guess it's sort of like a mistake that can be fixed. One day they'll be the right ones.

(More intellectual tone — he's thought this through.)

Of the two options for female-to-male sex reassignment surgery, neither sound really good...but if anything, it would be metaoidioplasty (clit-release) because you keep the feeling in it, can still get it up, not as expensive, not as many operations, and not as many complications.

(Excited.) I heard people that for people taking testosterone, it makes their clits look like little cocks. I also heard that licorice was a natural androgen. Licorice is THE DEVIL! The most nastiest-tasting thing in the world. But I made myself eat it! I don't know if I expected to grow a dick or what...nothing changed.

I haven't lost my virginity yet. It would be too weird, using this...I'd either have to do someone with a strap-on, or get it up the ass, or give it orally, but I can't even get used to the idea of having one...I couldn't let someone stick something up it.

The only sexual activities I've ever done were in role-playing games, written on paper, where I've always been male and done stuff with a dick. On paper, the ones I have don't matter. On paper, I can have anything.

A DYKE WITH A DYCK

By Lauren W. Steely

LAUREN, a Transgender Woman, 22 years old

LAUREN enters with a water bottle and fashionable book bag, like a young, hip teacher. She takes a folder out of the bag, opens it, and organizes her notes. She removes a lint catcher from her bag and runs it over her clothes, then takes a sip from her water bottle before focusing her attention on the audience. You can almost hear the "Good morning, class." Smiling, confident.

I'm a 22-year-old, Caucasian, pansexual genderqueer dyke who used to be a straight and narrow guy, but now, thankfully, has evolved. These days I am a graduate student in the earth sciences at a large university in California...but I'm originally an east coast kid from Maryland.

(Pause, thinking about how to describe her body.)

The short answer is, I am a dyke with a dyck. Now that's D-Y-C-K.

(Writes it on the board in huge capital letters.)

But it didn't always used to be this way.

I used to have a pretty normal set of "male" genitalia.

(Draws cartoonish male genitals on the board.)

I never used the words cock, dick, or balls because they sounded too macho and sexually aggressive. I was a straight guy and I enjoyed my penis though I never used it for its "intended" purpose.

When I moved to California and decided to go on estrogen and grow my hair out, the way I thought about things started to change. I made no pretenses about having always been a woman. I didn't particularly care if anyone read me as such. And I was ambivalent about genital surgery. But still I wanted a more female body.

(Draws curvy female outline on the board.)

It's not that I hated my penis, or felt that it was wrong on me. But I would have gladly exchanged it for a cunt, if only so I could do all the usual dyke things in bed with another woman.

(Moves to draw, then stops, laughing, and erases it. She shakes a finger — naughty — at the audience. She's playing with us to put us at ease.)

So I asked my girlfriends to ignore it or treat it as a large clit, and this worked out pretty well. I never used it for penetration though: that felt too male.

Pretty soon I started hanging out with other dykes at school and I began to identify very strongly as a lesbian, becoming very absorbed in the culture and community. As much as I wanted a cunt, I began to see my existing genitals as kind of an asset in the dyke world: it's like a having a permanent strap-on.

So, after a year of desperately wanting a cunt and leaning ever more toward surgery, I'm finally becoming comfortable with my dyck.

(As though responding to a question from the audience.)

What changed? *(Pause.)* Well, since then I've read a lot of erotica, read a lot of boundary-shattering queer essays, looked at a lot of dyke porn, and become ever more acquainted with the wonderfully rich spectrum of female masculinities that are flooding the dyke community these days — FtMs, tranny boyz, faggot-identified dykes, butches of all flavors.

Now this is the beauty of growing up in this very queer and very revolutionary time...I've had so many images presented to me of dykes with cocks, dykes wanting their own real cocks, dykes craving other women's and men's cocks, dykes sucking cocks, etc., that it's not so incongruous anymore that I have one. Like I said, I'm even coming to see it as a unique advantage. Hence the fact that, within my own schema of subversive semantic queering, I had to change the spelling....

(Returns to the board.)

Repeat after me it's not D-I-C-K, *(writes D-I-C-K)* it's D-Y-C-K.

(Underlines the "Y," crosses out the word "dick.")

For exactly the same reason that it's womyn and not woman.

(Writes on the board to show difference, crosses out the word "woman.")

Good job, class.

(Back to lecturing.) Traditional cultural semiotics dictates that a dick signifies masculinity, virility, machismo, dominance, power. Why not create a new, queer semiotics? One where a dyck can signify womanhood, dykehood, genderqueerhood, or anything else one might imagine?

It doesn't even have to be gendered at all.

(Thundering theory — mocking her own language.)

In a perfect world, we'd all realize that the problem all too often lies with culturally-constructed, naturalized semiotic systems rather than with our own bodies or minds.

(Slowly, more seriously — this is important.)

And yet, I acknowledge that in a perfect world, there would still be people who want to change their bodies and minds, in the absence of any cultural imperative to do so. Because each of us has our own tastes and preferences and identities. *(With finality.)* And that's all this gender stuff should be: a preference, an affinity.

(Packs up her things, then reminds us, the nervous scholars:)

And yes, that will be on the final exam.

(Exits.)

AN AVERAGE BLOKE
By Graeme

GRAEME, a Straight, Cisgender man in his mid-30s

GRAEME enters awkwardly, greets individual audience members. Shakes a few hands shyly. Not really sure what to say. He has a slight Scottish accent.

Hi there. My name is Graeme. *(Pause.)* I'm just an average bloke. I work at a call center. It's not the best job, but it pays the bills. *(Pause.)* I just got married a few months ago, moved from Scotland to San Francisco.

(Pause, unsure how to go on.)

I haven't a clue about gender, to be honest. It's not something I really need to think about.

(Pause. Searching his brain, then comes up with this example.)

When I was a wee kid, I thought I used to be a girl. And not in the "past life" sense, either; I actually thought I'd been born a girl, and then my mum and dad had decided that I'd be better off as a boy and put me through some kind of baby gender change operation. I had reasons for this, of course; my sister, all of eleven months older than me, had overheard my parents talking about what turned out to be my circumcision but only understood that SOMETHING had happened and it meant that someone had done some kind of operation "down there," as she put it. And my mum and dad had always told me how they'd really wanted a boy, and I put the two things together in my head and came up with the gender swap theory. I can't remember how long it lasted — not THAT long, I don't think, maybe a couple of months or so — but eventually I plucked up enough courage to ask my mum, who promptly told me I was talking rubbish and that

I'd always been a boy and that I didn't have to know what the operation down there was about right then, anyway.

So, that was that.

(Remembering, picking up speed.)

But later, at school, I never did any of the traditional "boy" things. I was shite at football. I didn't like the pissing contests that my friends got up to in the school toilets, streams of piss fighting and flying into each other like lightsabers at half-ten in the morning. I couldn't tell anyone anything about cars or army comics or anything like that, and where I came from, that was all that seven-year-old boys were into... So I hung out with the girls instead. I was used to being around them because of my two sisters, and I ended up getting called an "honorary girl," *(Pause.)* a title that kept popping up throughout my life, usually when I'd listen to a female friend bitching about her relationship troubles.

(Thinking again, new example.)

Years later than that and I'm fourteen and learning about sex from my Dad's porn magazines and trying to work out what I'm into and what I'm not, and I steal my sister's clothes and try them on to see if it does anything for me. I put on stolen lipstick and bad blusher and tear tights to shreds with toenails that need to be cut. Leg hairs poking through everywhere...I sit and look at myself in the mirror and I don't look like anything, especially not anything arousing. My transvestite period lasted about four attempts across two weeks.

(Thinking again.)

From there to age 20, and my then-girlfriend Tina sitting up in bed after we'd fucked, looking down at me, squinting through the smoke: "Sometimes I think I'm more of a man than you are," she said before adding, "mind you, could say that about most of the men I know."

(Pause, thinking again. Draws a blank, apologetically.)

So. That's all I can think of. I guess my story's a bit rubbish compared to some...

(Finality. Apologetic, feels he's wasted our time.)

It's probably not what you wanted. I'm sorry I couldn't be more helpful.

(Awkwardly salutes the people he greeted. Exits with a few shy "goodbyes.")

DOCTOR
By Lauren W. Steely

LAUREN, a Transgender Woman in her early 20s

Lights up on LAUREN sitting on the table. Her tone is familiar, as though telling a story to a friend.

So I'm sitting on an examination table in my doctor's office in LA. The male nurse who is going to give me my preliminary physical walks in — a young, very attractive black man who steals glances at me while he asks me questions and writes on his clipboard.

"And you're...going from...a man...to...a woman? Is that right?" I love that he can't tell. Guess he isn't too sure what he'll find down there, but he's obviously attracted to me. He's curious how long I've been on hormones.

"About 11 months," I smile.

"That recently?" He's amazed. "And gosh, you're so pretty!"

I'm starting to like this guy.

Finally he asks me to take off my shirt and lie down. He shows me how to examine my new breasts for lumps. Then comes the testicular exam. I am fairly certain he has never done both of these exams back to back before. That thought makes me smile.

I pull off my boxers and he takes a good look and tries to be professional about it, but I can tell that he's still kind of in disbelief.

As I am buttoning up my shirt, he gets around to awkwardly asking me about my sexual habits. I can see the question coming from a mile away, so I just interrupt him matter-of-factly—"I'm a virgin."

He gives me another amused, amazed look of disbelief: "You're still a virgin, looking like that...!" I almost laugh out loud. It's an entirely inappropriate thing to say, of course, and every feminist fiber in my body twitches, but I don't mind. It's clear that he doesn't think of me in androgynous terms, like most people...he sees me as a cute girl who happens to have a penis. And somehow his mind is able to reconcile these two facts unproblematically. I wish I could do it so easily.

THE MISSING VAGINA MONOLOGUE
By Esther Morris Leidolf

ESTHER, an Intersex Woman, 3 DOCTORS, LOVER (Can be played by the same actor as one of the Doctors.)

NOTE: No DOCTOR should ever directly address ESTHER. To them she is a fascinating medical condition, not a human being.

ESTHER walks over and lies down on the table. DOCTOR 3 puts a sheet over her lower body, as for a gynecological exam. He peeks under sheet, calls in the other 2 DOCTORS. They are all dressed in white lab coats. Scribbling away with excitement at their medical discoveries, they examine her, then pull away and huddle to consult each other. ESTHER sits up and addresses the audience.

ESTHER:	My life is about to change forever. I am thirteen-years-old, and I got sent home from camp with abdominal pain. I have just had surgery, because they thought my hymen was closed and keeping the blood from getting out. But now these doctors tell me I don't have a vagina and maybe no uterus. They label me with
DOCTOR 1:	*(Popping out of the huddle, as an exclamation.)* Sexual dysfunction!
ESTHER:	*(Sarcastically.)* because I can't have *intercourse* without a vagina. My doctors recommend vaginal reconstruction so I can have a normal sex life with my husband when I get married.

(She holds herself protectively. Very small and alone.)

I am 13 years old — what does all this mean to me? All I wanted to do was go water skiing.

I spent the next few years going to specialists, *(Stands, walks to DOCTORS. They surround her, taking her pulse, heartbeat, etc.)* having tests to confirm my gender, being probed by curious doctors and interns with multiple instruments in multiple holes at multiple times.

DOCTOR 2:   Say AH.

(He takes a sample from inside of her cheek. ESTHER lets him finish, then tears herself away from them — almost violently — and returns to the table.)

ESTHER: There were no women doctors involved in any of my treatment. My chromosomes were counted and discussed in front of me.

DOCTOR 2:   Got to run that test again just to make sure.

ESTHER: There were not enough other signs to determine gender for these guys.

(DOCTORS surround her at the table, replacing the sheet when she lies down. DOCTOR 2 examines her breasts while DOCTORS 1 and 3 take eager notes between her legs.)

ESTHER: They examined my breasts, labia, clitoris, with blind eyes. They had their definition of normal, and I wasn't it. There was so much focus on the woman I "should be" that I lost all knowledge of the girl that I was.

(DOCTOR 1 holds up XX clipboard.)

> Once I was officially determined female my reconstruction was arranged. Then I could adopt children and life would be just fine. At age fifteen I had my second and third surgeries.

(She lies down on the table, DOCTORS spread the sheet over her lower body. DOCTORS 1 and 2 don surgical masks. DOCTOR 2 mimes "surgery" between her legs, with DOCTOR 1 assisting, as DOCTOR 3 describes the procedure.)

DOCTOR 3:   ...a slight dimple is present where the vagina should be. By means of sharp and blunt dissection a very adequate vagina will be developed...a skin graft will be obtained from the buttocks, attached to the mold, and inserted into the cavity...The vagina will be closed...all sponges will be accounted for.

(DOCTORS go back to their huddle, stripping off masks and congratulating each other silently on a job well done. ESTHER sits up and turns to the audience again.)

ESTHER: I was given vaginal dilators for postoperative therapy, to keep my vagina *functional*. A functional vagina is

DOCTOR 1:   A vagina that will be able to accept a normal size penis.

(DOCTOR 3 hands dilator to her. She studies it for a minute.)

ESTHER: I am 15 years old.

DOCTOR 2:   Just use it like a shoe stretcher.

(DOCTORS exit.)

ESTHER: The problem was solved, for everyone but me.

I was another surgical success.

(LOVER enters. She turns to face him, still sitting on the table, side to the audience. They embrace – things get steamy. His face is buried in her chest, arms groping at her back. She reaches down between them, mechanically, almost violently jerking him off. She speaks around him.)

ESTHER: Two years later I started having sex. After all that trouble I discovered that a penis would respond to anything.

(LOVER comes — a moan. ESTHER wipes her hand on the table behind her in disgust. She angrily pushes the LOVER away. He exits.)

I felt abused in the most intangible way, a victim of arrogance and assumption. I became an instant survivor.

Tidbits of emotion overwhelmed me in very big ways. I alienated myself from peers who would rightfully complain of menstrual cramps and *(screams at a woman in the audience)* no! I don't have a tampon!

I wish I could have had choices...

(ESTHER returns to the podium, becomes a public speaker once again. The rest of the piece is a powerful speech.)

Why was my gender challenged in the first place, and then confirmed like something

28

I didn't already know? My breasts, my clit, my labia, my feelings mean nothing because I'm missing a vagina? Why was my body taken away and rearranged like a sexual Action Figure by men with knives? What was the need to feminize my body? They have neutered my soul!

As I grow older I am faced with even more questions. How will I experience menopause? How do I monitor my ovaries? How many ovaries do I have and where are they hiding? What about pap smears? My sister is the one who told me there was an actual name for my condition: Mayer-Rokitansky-Kuster-Hauser syndrome. That is when I discovered the other symptoms associated with my Syndrome, which explained the years of disability and hearing loss. Had I known my condition made me more susceptible to physical disability, I would have made different decisions. But everyone was too focused on the hole, or lack thereof, to pay any attention to the person.

I have read a lot about the "medical challenge" of treating women with vaginal agenesis but I think the challenge is broader than that. We challenge the role presented to women and that makes people very nervous. We challenge the concept of normal for gender and sexual activity, and that makes people fanatic. We are literally molded to fit societal values. This isn't just about bodies it is about genocide of variation.

(ESTHER steps out from behind the podium, walks towards audience again. She stops center stage, and delivers the rest of her speech directly to the audience.)

I come out about my surgery in carefully selected ways. I have seen the response of too many twisted faces. They show me pity. One medical practitioner told me I was "just too weird." Lesbians who were born with vaginas have asked me "is this what made you a lesbian?"

I want people to understand that doing the right thing often does more harm than good. The standard of normal that we aim for is imaginary. People don't fail to meet the definitions of normal gender, but the definitions fail to meet the people. Being born without a vagina was not my problem. Having to get one was the real problem. My "sexual dysfunction" posed less of a threat to my health than the parts of the Syndrome that disabled me. So why is a vagina all I was given to cope with a much greater loss?

http://www.mrkh.org/

DICK

By Elaine "Lannie" Rose and Daniel

LANNIE, a Transgender Woman, DANIEL, a Transgender Man

LANNIE sits on one end of the table, DANIEL on the other. They face diagonally out into different sides of the audience. They are unaware of each other's presence — these are simultaneous, overlapping monologues. LANNIE is animated and humorous, DANIEL is quiet and poetic. They serve as sharp contrasts to each other, with LANNIE's rapid banter swirling around DANIEL's quiet reflections.

LANNIE: I'm a chick with a dick. But I would rather be a chick with a vagina.

DANIEL: Before I started testosterone, I hadn't realized how numb I was.

LANNIE: I was born with a dick. I knew how to use it. I used it at every opportunity. I am pleased to report that my dick works.

DANIEL: I didn't so much realize this at the time, but a mouth on my clit could make me gasp with wanting, with reaching...for something that was never quite there.

LANNIE: A little while ago, I decided to live the rest of my life as a woman. The question is, what do I do about my dick?

DANIEL: I didn't want to be touched unless I was already close to the edge. I would push people away — not yet, wait, a little longer. I didn't want a hand in the space that arcs away from my center, the space that should be filled with nerves and skin.

31

Touch, instead, the base, where cock
meets flesh, let the rest of me strain out,
phantom skin, phantom touch.

LANNIE: I'm surprised at how many men like my
dick. Back when I was a man, I would
have been appalled to find a dick on a
woman. Now I'm pretty broad-minded
about it, and so are a lot of other people it
seems. And I guess some people are just
kinky.

DANIEL: I was scared that taking T wasn't going to
be enough. Somewhere in the first two
months, though, I grew a dick. It wasn't
the size — although it's nice to see
something arcing away from my body,
even if only for an inch or so. Rather, my
whole response changed. I get hard, and I
can watch my dick grow. I can feel a thick
cylinder; pull back the hood to see the
head and part of the shaft. I can grab onto
it, tug it. It doesn't feel like the same piece
of flesh.

LANNIE: Back when I was a man, my dick worked
liked this: if I saw a beautiful woman, my
dick would start to get hard. If she had
big, beautiful, rounded breasts, blood
would rush into my dick, and it would get
bigger. If those breasts were exposed, or
nipples were evident, my dick would get
even bigger and harder. If I saw a pretty
woman with long shapely legs and a short
skirt, dick again. If I thought I could get a
glance up that skirt when she sat down,
big-time dick!

DANIEL: It's easy to call it a dick now. Before I
started T, it always sounded forced. But it

doesn't feel like dreaming or denial or dysphoria. Dick feels like just the right word.

LANNIE: Nowadays, if I see a beautiful woman, I check out her shoes. If they're cute, I want to know where she got them. If she has big breasts and a nice ass, I will admire them, even be jealous, but it does not cause blood to pump into my dick. I'm not sure why. I would still like to make love to a beautiful woman. I just haven't had the opportunity for several years. Maybe it seems so unobtainable to me, that my dick can't be bothered to make the effort.

DANIEL: I hadn't realized before how numb I was.

LANNIE: I do make love with men these days. But the sight of a tall, strong, handsome guy does not send the blood rushing into my dick. Sometimes when I let myself imagine how nice it will feel when he is holding me, stroking me, wanting me...that can cause a dick uprising, indeed. Usually I try not to let that happen, because I don't like the sight of my dick tenting the skirt of my dress.

DANIEL: I find my hand wandering between my legs at random times. Not to jerk off, exactly, but just to stroke along its length, feel the rush of blood, the texture of fabric against the head.

LANNIE: When I make love with a man, I love his dick. I like to hold it; I like to feel it grow in my hand, or my mouth. I like to suck on it and hear him groan.

DANIEL: I had hoped I would grow big enough to overcome the dysphoria. Instead — I care less what I *think* about my dick, because, for the first time, I can feel it.

LANNIE: Often guys want to grab my crotch, feel my cock, suck on my dick. I don't get it. I don't want to suck on a woman's dick. I guess I don't get why I don't get it, as well. I like sucking on theirs, why shouldn't they like sucking on mine? Because I'm a woman, dammit! Maybe somehow it makes me feel like less of one.

DANIEL: Sometimes my own body even turns me on.

LANNIE: I sometimes let guys do what they want with my dick. I mean, if they really dig it, then it's okay with me. I love the attention. And yes, it feels really good. Sometimes I even cum.

DANIEL: Even bare flesh feels new to me.

LANNIE: I don't let guys fuck me in the ass. I wish I could, but my asshole is just too damn tight. I'm working on it. Maybe someday I'll be able to do that. I've had things in my ass, and I know it can be a wonderful sensation. And it's not un-womanly, you know. Some women take it in the ass. Hell, I've seen them do it in movies!

DANIEL: I am rediscovering having sex naked.

LANNIE: So far, nobody has been upset that I won't let them fuck me in the ass. I'm pretty selective about who I have sex with, and besides, there's plenty of other fun things to do.

DANIEL: I am rediscovering the blow job.

LANNIE: The other night I was making love with my boyfriend. I was lying on top of him; not supporting my torso on my arms, like a man would, but laying all my weight on him in a big hug. I got to moving my hips so my erect penis rubbed in his groin. I closed my eyes. He held me tightly and, just with the warmth of his embrace, encouraged me to enjoy myself. I drifted away, and shed a few tears of happiness as I came.

DANIEL: My lover takes his time from my chest to my belly, and I silently urge him to hurry up. I want to feel his mouth on my cock. When he finally takes me into his mouth, sucks my dick longer, presses it between his tongue and the roof of his mouth, I can feel every millimeter. I feel my cock straining to meet him. Nothing phantom here, just swollen skin and a warm encircling tongue. Within seconds I am close to coming, but I don't want to come. I just want to lie here, one hand on his ear, the other curled around the back of his neck, and feel his mouth and his breath on me. I don't want to come, because I don't want him to stop.

LANNIE: But even as I enjoyed it, I wished that, instead of a penis, I had a vagina. I wished his penis could be throbbing and erect inside my vagina, and the shaft of it rubbing on my clitoris, creating the sensations I was feeling in my body.

DANIEL:

I relax into his mouth, growing with his grip. He pulls away for a moment, sucking as his mouth releases me, and I lift my hips to follow him. The air is cold, sudden, and I can still feel his mouth on me. He bends his head to meet me, swallowing me, lets go. I throb. He covers my dick again with his mouth, touches the head with the tip of his tongue, presses lightly. My muscles spasm, and I ejaculate onto his chin and neck, onto the bed. I clench and unclench my fingers. I beg him not to stop.

LANNIE:

So that's really why I want a vagina. Yes, tucking is a pain in the ass (sometimes literally). And it's awkward if my dick flops out of my panties and dangles around under my skirt. It would be nice to wear a bikini bottom at the pool. But mostly, I want to make love as a woman. Not as a chick with a dick.

PEE

GENDER FREAK

Lights up onstage and in the house. The FREAK enters, walks center stage, speaks directly to the audience.

How you all doing? Enjoying the play? Feeling stimulated? Good. Glad to hear it. So, I have a question for you...do any of you have to pee? Raise your hands, don't be shy. I know I do.

Excuse me for a sec.

(Moves to table, sits. Crosses legs, holds them tightly together with one hand.)

That's better. Seriously, this is an ongoing problem. I've given myself three urinary tract infections in two months! One time I even wet myself...and ya know why?

(Pause, looks out at audience, smiles, finds an ally.)

Yeah, I bet you know why. I mean, look at me? What do you think they see? Well, that little old lady in Costco sure saw a big scary man...she called the cops on me!

(Looks at audience again, picks a new ally.)

You know what I mean...such a fucking shame. No place to pee. Last week my friend was raped by the security guards for being in the "wrong" bathroom. And did you read the paper? "Transvestite stabbed in men's room." Makes my bladder infection seem pretty tame, doesn't it? I mean, how degrading is this? To take away our right to piss. We give our cats a litter box, we take our dogs for walks, even the fucking canary gets a fucking newspaper.

(Stands on table, authoritative pose. FREAK should work to ensure audience participation at this point — ad-libbing as necessary.)

OK, I want another show of hands: who here has ever gone for a day without peeing? Raise 'em up if you run away from the little skirt woman or the little pants man when you're out in the world. If you've ever walked to a different floor, or a different building, or all the way back home to find a safe bathroom.

(Studies the audience for a while.)

That's too fucking many. And it has to fucking stop.
(Pause.)

And now, my friends, enjoy your intermission. For your convenience, the bathrooms have been degendered tonight! So please, pee safely! Pee comfortably. Enjoy your pee. But wait — me first!

(Rushes out of the room.)

END OF ACT ONE

RADICAL COCK

A GENDER FREAK, hir silent FANTASY WOMAN

FREAK enters from the back of the audience and makes hir way to the stage. Ze is loud and confident, clad in vinyl. Ze speaks to the audience, toys with it, taunts it.

I like to be radical. I like to use harsh words like fuck and cunt, or intellectual queer theory words like binary or dysphoria. I like to fuck shit up. Down with the gender system! Fuck gender! Fuck society! Fuck oppressors. *(To audience member.)* Are you an oppressor? Fuck you! *(Double flip off.)*

(By now ze is onstage, strutting hir stuff.)

I like my sex life to be radical. I like to fuck the kind of people where the whole world wonders "is that a boy or a girl?"

(Picks a member of the audience.)

Yeah, like you.

(Seductive/dominating tone. FREAK approaches the victim, purring into hir ear.)

I'd like to take you home with me and make sure not even you can ever tell again.

(Climbs up and stands on the table.)

I'm a female-bodied queer faggot top genderfuck punk, and don't you ever forget it. *(Pointing at audience member.)* I know you won't. I like to keep people guessing, and make sure they want me anyway. *(To another audience member, seductively.)* Are you guessing? Can you tell? *(Pause.)* Don't you want me anyway?

(Laughs.) What a rush of power.

I'll fuck anybody, any way. *(To audience member.)* Especially you. With whatever outrageous toys you want, any scenario, nothing's too weird.

(Runs hands up and down hir own body, radical porn star style.)

I revel in my body. In its holes, its bones, its muscles. I know what I want and I know how to get it. *(Loudly.)* You can stick a nine-inch dildo in me — and I'm talking diameter — *(Indicates size with hands by making a circle with thumbs and index fingers.)* and fuck me until I pass out. No problem. My cunt is fine. *(Shouts.)* I like to fuck shit up.

(Shift, quieter...more intimate in a personal sense. Sits down on the table, looks down, a little bit ashamed. Still a little seductive, but more honest.)

But I have a secret.

Sometimes, I just want a cock.

(This to separate members of the audience as though recalling their shared experience with these toys.)

No, not the red and black marbled one, or the one shaped like a dolphin, or the violet one that vibrates, or even the super realistic "real flesh sensation" one that comes complete with balls and bulging veins...

(Walks around, stands behind table.)

No. Sometimes, I just want a real cock, attached to me.

(Presses hir groin into the back of the table, palms down on its surface.)

I want to feel it harden when I'm aroused, to press it against my lovers, to feel it push inside them. *(Closes eyes, arches back.)* Just once, I'd like to know what a blow job feels like. What it feels like to have my dick enveloped by a willing throat. *(Opens eyes, to audience.)* And it's not just gay porn fantasies of making some boy bend over in a dark alley and feeling his ass give in to my pulsating member. *(Points to audience member.)* I know you were thinking that. No, this is serious.

My secret is more shameful than that.

(FANTASY WOMAN enters, in revealing lingerie. Long blond hair, big breasts, boots. A seductive strut. FREAK looks at her, and acknowledges her, as she slowly approaches the table.)

Sometimes, I would like to have a cock, and to make love with it, in every slow, sickening Hollywood detail.

(FANTASY WOMAN moves to the table, lies down, her hair spilling over the end, legs spread.)

To be a sickeningly straight man, making love with a sickeningly straight woman.

(FREAK climbs onto the table, moves between her legs as if penetrating her.)

My stubble on her smooth cheek. My hair short, hers long, bulging pectorals pressing into her soft breasts.

(Stagehand throws a blanket over them — it covers their waists and legs as they simulate heterosexual intercourse — missionary position. FREAK's words build in speed and intensity with hir thrusts.)

I'd like to slide gently into her, missionary position, feel myself inside her, and on top of her, feel her muscles and soft wetness around me, and make us both come so quietly and gently and heterosexually *(Pause — they come.)* that it makes me sick to admit it.

FREAK sits up between FANTASY WOMAN's legs, pulling the blanket around hir shoulders as if covering hir nudity. Ze suddenly looks very small. FANTASY WOMAN lies motionless, her legs still spread, face turned away from the audience.

What do you think of me now, huh? What kind of radical do you see? Where's all that power now? All that *(Hits the sociology word hard, long.)* agency? Am I just a victim of the mass media? What kind of radical wants to be the patriarchy?

Looks down at FANTASY WOMAN, runs hir fingers slowly up her bare thigh before looking back out at the audience.

Then again, maybe that's a pretty radical idea after all.

BLEEDING
By Daniel

DANIEL, a Transgender Man

Lights up on DANIEL leaning against the table. He has been asked — by a stranger, perhaps a doctor of some kind — to describe his experiences with menstruation.

Menstruation? You want me to talk about *(Drawn-out medical word.)* menstruation? Let me think for a minute...

(He begins seriously, remembering with some disbelief that anyone could be so happy about bleeding.)

OK. I once dated a woman who was in love with menstruating. She never was quite able to articulate why, but as soon as she started bleeding, she'd ricochet around, hyper and happy and telling the world how much she loved her period.

Come to think of it, the first time I slept with her, she was bleeding. We drank in my dorm room and shyly pressed our bare feet together. We had sex in her room until about seven in the morning. A drunken and joyous sort of sex — that rare kind in which first-time awkwardness and beer-induced numbness don't get in the way.

The sun came up and lit on her sheets, once white, now splashed and spreading with blood. It faded quickly from the bright red, a fainter and fainter brown each time the sheets were washed.

(Smile, somewhat bold, looking the audience in the eye.)

I had bitten bruises up and down her torso. They faded, too, from dark red to blue to green and yellow, until we made bruises again.

(Beat. Forcing himself to make it personal. This is not his favorite subject, nor is it excruciatingly painful. It is a part of his past that he wishes hadn't been necessary but has accepted all the same.)

OK. Back to the subject at hand.

(Looks down his body.)

The first time, the blood was thick and brown. I knew what was happening — I'd read about it, felt, as I did with most of these bodily changes, neither pleased nor despairing. I did not want to tell anyone, or make a mess. I rummaged in the bathroom for pads, and I wadded the stained underwear up into a ball and threw it into the hamper.

(Pause — how much peace has he really found? This is peace in the sense of "dealing with," not in the sense of harmony.)

I found my peace with menstruation through a myth about women, in the days before writing and patriarchy, revered and feared because they bled for a week and did not die. Menstruating not as shame, but as mysterious strength.

(Pause. Almost a nod.)

This I could do.

I could bleed and bleed, and marvel at how it did not kill me.

(Picking up speed, explaining carefully — this is why it was so bad.)

I didn't hate menstruating, but I was ready to be done with it. The incongruity of blood stains on my men's briefs. How can he bleed there and not be hurt?

I would forget for hours at a time, *(This is key.)* but in the forgetting I was also forgetting my body, my genitals. I stopped having sex on the days when I was bleeding.

The disconnection was growing, my body becoming a stranger as I began to envision what I could draw myself into.

Like a rip in my skin, who my body claimed I was, who I was, what my body could become. Holding silent when I was passing, so my voice would not give me away. *(Pause.)* The rich scent of blood in the men's room.

After I started taking testosterone, I bled only once, and then I was done.

(Pulls himself together, back to the present, runs his hands along his body to assure himself of his presence now.)

Now my body harbors new mysteries. I pierce my skin with a needle every ten days — a drop of blood welling up. I feel the testosterone flowing through my body.

(Mimes stabbing his leg.)

The slow process of making it mine.

(Runs hands across his flat chest.)

My skin tight across new muscle — scratch it open, and I bleed.

But only then.

TRANSPARENT

JIM, a young boy, SCHOOL NURSE

JIM sits on the table — an examination table in the SCHOOL NURSE's office. He is holding his stomach; the NURSE is feeling his forehead.

NURSE: Well, Jim, it looks like you've got a pretty bad flu. I think we should call and see which one of your parents can come pick you up. Is that a good idea?

(JIM nods pathetically.)

NURSE: Who should we call?

JIM: My mom.

NURSE: Ok, will she be able to come pick you up right away?

JIM: He.

(NURSE is distracted — rummaging through her files for JIM's mom's phone number.)

NURSE: What's that dear?

JIM: He. My mom prefers to be called *he*.

(NURSE smiles nervously — doesn't know how to respond. Holds up information sheet with the parental contact info.)

NURSE: Here we go. Now, Jim, I don't understand...there's no mom listed here. Just two men. Robert and John Thompson.

JIM: That's what I'm telling you. My mom's new name is John. He likes to be called he. Could you please call him? I really don't feel good.

NURSE: Now, I think we need to sort things out first. I don't want to call just anyone. Maybe there's been a mistake at the office. *(To herself.)* Could the mother's name be *Joan*?

(JIM is getting more and more pathetic and sick.)

JIM: No mistake. Those are my parents. Robert is my dad and John is my mom. *(Urgently.)* Please call him!

NURSE: This is so peculiar. *(Has an epiphany, turns on her PC charm.)* Oh, I see. Jimmy *(JIM hates being called "Jimmy.")*, do you have two daddies? Isn't that nice. Well, which one should we call to pick you up?

JIM: *(Really fed up.)* Listen! I'm sick. I don't have two dads. I have a dad and a mom. Please call my mom. His name is John Thompson and I want him to come pick me up.

NURSE: I don't understand.

JIM: I just want my mom!!!

DAS TYLE
By tyle fernández

TYLE, a Genderqueer person.

Lights up on TYLE, leaning against the wall, John-Wayne style, with one foot up.

Most people probably assume I have a penis because of the way I look. Do you? They say something like, "Yeah, you're a guy!" I ask them how they can be so sure. "Well, you are, aren't you; I mean you have a, uh..." and I raise my eyebrows and frown, adding tension to the rising suspicion. They're strangely not satisfied until I relent and acknowledge that "Yes, I'm a man," which they ironically assume to mean that I have a penis, although I still haven't said for sure whether I have!

(Crosses to table, leans onto it from behind, lounging.)

I'm transgender because gender is always on my mind. It's a bit of an unhealthy obsession, really, being multi-gendered.

(Walks to the front of the table, the sort of pacing walk that indicates thought.)

I've learned to identify with and embrace most labels that one could chuck at my head — queer, gay, bisexual, multi-sexual, boy, dyke, fag, drag queen, boygirl, transgender.... But never "man," never "heterosexual," and always simply, tyle. That's my name. Like the ones in the bathroom, but with a "y." tyle.

In the German language, which I'm beginning to fluently embrace as my own, one often uses a gendered "the" when referring to a person, such as "ask the Jessica" instead of simply "ask Jessica." They use the masculine form for me, but I correct them, saying that tyle is always neutral; please say "das tyle," not "der tyle." Danke.

But they usually don't get it and try to educate this strange American foreign exchange student about proper German grammar usage. I understand it all too well already.

I started identifying as transgender when I stopped thinking of myself as male. Outwardly I'm a rather traditionally masculine type. But even though I'm ghastly to behold in a wig and false eyelashes (Madame Bizarre, they call me),

(Good-natured, mocking presentation for the following: runs hands up leg for "fishnets," adjusts the imaginary wig, kicks up the "high heels," and turns to show off his butt in the imaginary miniskirt.)

I fear no shame in skirting gender through donning fishnets, a red wig and high heels in a skimpy pleather miniskirt. Although that's for show, I also feel comfortable wearing a long black skirt into town to the supermarket on a regular day.

I don't alter my gender presentation based on people's assumptions of my genitals. And I don't tuck and tape when in a tight skirt. *(Grabbing crotch.)* Let it bulge, for heaven's sake. Girls have dicks too!

(Sits on table, leans back, remembering. Gets carried away with stories — doesn't mean to mention the video camera. His embarrassment is obvious and endearing.)

Me and my genitals, we go way back. We used to sit around the fire together, go biking unfettered in the forest, jog on the treadmill, perform for the video camera.

I have a penis. I also have an anus that is very much like a vagina. Receptive to penises and other such toys. Within it sleeps a pleasure that can be aroused by the right fingers, and sometimes it's hungry. Sometimes it wants to get out and play.

Yes, but it's not really the cleanest place in the world. At least with a rear-vagina you don't have to worry about getting pregnant. So my manpussy does have its advantages.

I don't like to use genitals as instruments of a sexual act. I like them to be pleased as a part of a person, but not The Only Part that deserves attention, and preferably fitted into a more romantic and less pornographic setting. This one guy said "feed it to me" and I lost my erection trying to control my laughter. The image of a penis soufflé or something still won't leave my mind.

I've often thought I might get a sex change when I'm 80. I'll have inhabited this masculine body for long enough, and I believe I'll be ready to put a new spin on things. I'd rather be a feisty old woman than a rumpled old man. I want to be the grand old mother of the family, revered for her inclusiveness. Besides, won't that thing down there shrivel up eventually anyway? Might as well slit it up the middle and tuck it inside and see what pleasure might be derived from a having a warm cave inside me. I wish I could have a baby. That'd be cool. Painful, but worth it.

Well, thanks to modern science, anyone who wants one can have a cute little vulva — anyone that is, who's willing to wait in line to convince the crackpots at the ministry of psychological stooges that it's okay to want to snip off your willy.

A boy can have a new vagina. He doesn't need to call himself a woman, unless she wants to. A biological woman can declare herself a man and keep his vagina.

In the same respect, a girl can have a new penis, a man can keep his penis, declare herself a woman, and no one should get upset about it.

AND THEN I MET YOU

ANTHONY, a Transgender Man in his early 20s

Lights up on ANTHONY sitting on the table. His arms are protectively around his knees, which are tucked up almost to his chin. He is a little embarrassed, talking to his current lover (the "you" later mentioned), but as he continues he grows bolder and more relaxed.

My first ideas of trans sex came from *Stone Butch Blues*. You know the title says it all really. I figured to be a good trans boy, a faithful butch, I had to be stone. Never let anyone in. That wasn't hard really, I was a petrified virgin. I had the best sexual defense mechanism ever: never let her touch me, be the tough, silent, stoic manly one. Do all for my lover and then turn away when her hands sought my skin under my clothes.

I wasn't very good at it. I liked orgasms too much, craved them even, as a way to finally connect to myself. But so often, I would panic when she touched me. Sometimes even the pressure of a well-meaning thigh against my boxer shorts was enough to make me turn away. Enough to make me need to get dressed. I needed layers between me and my lover. I needed to keep my body hidden away, I needed to be safe.

Time passed and I grew bolder. I got naked, let her hand touch me, learned not to panic when her bare skin brushed the hair down there...but there was always a sense of urgency. We developed a pattern: I would come first, then turn my attention to getting her off. What a relief to move on to her body! I would rush to come, be thankful when I managed it. Not sexual satisfaction so much as not having failed again.

Sometimes I did feel like lingering on my body, wanted us to focus on me, but how could I make her wait? How could I ask for something I was so ashamed I wanted? I fell asleep frustrated...a lot.

I came with my knees together; the word penetration wasn't even in my vocabulary.

And then I met you.

I didn't expect you to come along, but I was determined to do this relationship right. I had come a long way from stone. I had new friends, new sex positive trans friends, polyamorous and into leather. I had experimented, played with pain, even tried group fucking...but sex? Sex was still the same.

Your hand, my crotch, knees together. External sex. It was only a hole. A hole that bled when I didn't want it to, a hole that never did anything but embarrass me, a hole that wasn't supposed to be there. Boys don't have cunts, everyone knows that, and I wasn't about to challenge that idea.

And then I met you.

I don't know what changed. Maybe it was listening to all my radical trans friends who liked to get fucked, who bragged about the "extra tranny hole." Maybe it was the slew of penetration happy female bodied lovers I had. Maybe I just wanted to see what all the fuss was about.

Or maybe it was just you. Your non-judgmental eyes, hands, mouth and heart.

"You are a boy," you said to me once, "so you have a boy's body." It was that simple to you. It's still not that simple to me.

I don't remember how it happened. But one night your hand moved lower than usual and I didn't want you to stop. I asked you, tentatively, with my eyes, my noises, maybe even with words, to continue. You slid inside of me, so gently, so slowly, so different from the cold hands of the doctor, from my own fumbling hands, and from the harsh tubes of cotton that I forced up inside me every month. You were soft and living and warm, and I instantly wanted more.

That night I learned what all the fuss is about! You slipped past my walls of protection, my fear of my body, my fear of society, my idea of what boy means, and I came for you. You let me come. You fucked me until I couldn't speak, couldn't see, couldn't walk. I couldn't hide anymore, because you reached inside me and flipped my world upside down. And now I'm addicted to you.

THE CUTE GIRL WHO LIVES DOWN THE HALL
By Anonymous

CUTE GIRL, early 20s

"You" in this piece should never be generic. This character speaks to a friend/lover, a very specific person. Even if the entire audience is addressed as that person, it must never be a general thought. Honesty and coquettishness compete in her words and her attitude.

Lights up on CUTE GIRL sitting on the table, smiling sweetly out at the audience.

You know me. I'm the cute girl who lives down the hall.

(Sure of herself, seductively – she knows our deepest secrets.) You've always wanted to have sex with me, to lure me into your bedroom and strip off my clothes smiling.

You would want to kiss me. *(Pause)*

Eventually, you would want to slip your soft hands along my vagina,
(Seriously, cynically.) And I would feel obliged to move against you and show you how good it
felt,

(Her own need is taking over. She approaches the front row, and leans down into an audience member's face, delivering the next line only millimeters from her victim's lips.)

But I would want you to fuck me hard, so hard my skin would split, *(Pulling back a little, choosing a new victim.)* and I would want you to let me move against you, not thinking, doing what I must for that eventual release.

(Regains control, starts to walk back to the table. Throws a sweet glance over her shoulder at the audience, calls upon our intimacy.)

You know me.

(Gets up and lounges playfully on the table.)

You have even seen me naked, basking, lounging, teasingly unashamed of my body, of my pent-up
sensuality.

(Harshly.) You know very well that I have a vagina,
That I have been free with it in the past. *(Remembers.)*
(Bitterly.) They love being inside me,
Slow like honey, so intensely hot and slipping with the movement of my
hips.

(Pause, sadder memories now, still intimate. She almost cries.)

You know the weaknesses of my vagina.
How it will bleed, how I will pass out with pain.
You have held me up, you have been my comfort in my resentment,
You have fed me sips of water and kisses in my misery.
You know the weaknesses of my unsafe sexuality,
(Horror and pain in her voice.) You were as horrified as I at the changes in my body
when I tried to do right by my vagina
and took those horrid pills.

You have been patient with my infections and disease,

(Pause, this is it. Pulls herself together.)

But did you know how much I felt disconnected to the source of my discomfort?

(Kneels up on the table.)

You know how I am charged with sexual energy beyond that which can be
controlled,
(Shouting her frustration.) Do you know how queer I really am?
Do you know that when I am alone,
In my bed, asleep or very much awake,
In every fantasy I have ever recalled,
It is I who enter them,
I slip myself, my heat and desire, my hard longing,
Inside the soft kiss with which I am so familiar?

(Lies on her back on the table, as though having sex, showing us her struggle. Her movements build from the small gasp of "spasms" to the "uncontrollable movement" and tension of orgasm.)

My vagina has only ever really loved my fantasy.
It would appreciate the manipulations of well-meaning lovers,
But those spasms of joy, my real screams came only from my own thoughts.
I grind hard against myself,
A wrestling match of frustration and pure passion
Heat and wet uncontrollable movement, changing rhythms and my whole body tense,

(Orgasm — moaning and grasping — a full-body experience, then limp.)

Complete exhaustion afterwards,

(Sits up, lets her hair down, becomes playful, sweet, and almost shy with us.)

With lovers, kisses are my true release —
gender neutral sexual expression in its purest.

Kisses can melt me, Kisses can dizzy me,
Kisses have brought me to my knees.
My best lovers kiss my eager mouth while they fuck me,
And it is always the kisses that do it for me,
Not whatever they are doing with hands or tongues or toys
In that brown-seeming oh-so-wet deep-belly mouth between
my legs,

My vagina. *(Pause.)*
Vagina is the wrong word for it.
Genitals is wrong too.
Cunt is almost crude enough — something brusque and
forceful,
Inappropriate and dripping.

*(Stands up — back to seduction. During the following she
again enters the audience, touching and teasing various
members as though having the sex she describes.)*

Don't get me wrong — I love sex.
I adore sex.
I revel in sex.
I want to have sex all the time.
I once had sex for two days straight, taking turns.
I've had sex until we both bled, and kept on going.
I've had sex on mountaintops, in the ocean, and beneath
satin sheets.
I've had sex that tore and stained my clothes.
I've had sex until we were both dry, and a breeze made us
come.
I've had sex so wet that it soaked through blankets.
I've had sex with one person at a time, and with more than
one person.

*(She kicks the side of the table with her foot to produce a
rhythmic thumping noise, punctuating each of the following
words:)*

And I've had sex that disturbed the neighbors.
I've had sex in public.

I've had sex so slow it was hallucinatory.
I've had sex so rough I limped for days.
I've had sex that surprised me,
I've had sex that I planned,
I've had sex that embarrassed me,
I've had laughing sex.
And I'd have it all again.
I love sex.

*(Back to the table, leans against it. Her fingers on the
tabletop imitate what she describes.)*

I love the way other people's vaginas feel, taste, smell, look.
I love teasing, taunting, touching, tricking, and tantalizing
vaginas.
I love sliding my fingers barely over the softest skin,
I love making them lose control,
I love being in control.
I love finding myself inside unexpectedly,
I love pressing my leg hard into it all.
It has to be me, though.
Artificial sex organs are just that — artificial.
(To audience member.) My body longs for the chance to
make you scream unassisted.

(Proudly.) And my body does it well.
I have fucked every sort of vagina
I have fucked girl's vaginas, women's vaginas, and boy's
vaginas,
I have fucked vaginas that screamed with joy and vaginas
that whimpered in pain,
I have fucked a virgin and a whore,
and every one of those vaginas has loved me.

I would do anything to make a vagina happy.
It is because of the pleasure of their vaginas that I love sex.

And I have hope for my vagina being happy as well.
My new lover sees me not as the woman I am not,
But as the sexual being I am.

She kisses me as she wrestles with me,
She treats me with rough gentleness and gentle roughness,
She embraces my whole body rather than my vagina,
As I embrace her and hers.
I don't feel like a woman when I am with her,
Nor does she.
We just feel damned good,
Turned on, out of control, ecstatically happy,
Silly, and in love.
We choose not to define ourselves by our sex
But merely to have sex,
(Winking.) Lots of it,
(Serious.) And to enjoy it.

ELECTROLYSIS OF THE BALLS
By Elaine "Lannie" Rose

LANNIE, a Transgender Woman

Lights up on LANNIE sitting in a chair, as though on a talk show. Next to her is an empty chair in which sits the imaginary talk show host, whom she addresses sometimes. When the lights come up she is laughing, as though at something the host has just said. If her location seems unclear, a line such as "Oh Oprah, you're too much" may be added. She speaks with a Southern accent.

My mother persists in referring to my transsexuality as, "the lifestyle I have chosen to live." Right, Mom. I've chosen to be laughed at and ridiculed everywhere I go for the rest of my life. I don't mind that family members and close lifelong friends will no longer talk to me. I look forward to the series of painful and expensive surgeries. It's downright fun to tell every new boyfriend, "Dear, before we go any further, there's something I have to share with you...." Yep, this transsexual lifestyle is surely something people would jump at, if they only knew.

But I'll let you in on a secret. Those are not the worst part of being transsexual. Here is the dirty truth. The worst thing about being a transsexual is this: ELECTROLYSIS OF THE BALLS!!!

Oh, nobody likes to talk about that one. It's just too horrible to contemplate. But there it is.

When the surgeons construct my neovagina, they will use the skin of my scrotum to line its inner walls. Now nobody wants hair growing inside their vagina. It's uncomfortable and unhealthy. And damn hard to shave. Therefore, the scrotum must be made hairless prior to the operation. You do that by electrolysis.

Electrolysis hurts. They don't just poke needles into your skin. After they poke the needle in, they send a jolt of electrical charge into it. A charge strong enough to kill the hair follicle. It hurts when it's done on your chin. It hurts when it's done on your chest. It hurts like hell when it's done on your upper lip.

And, I've got to believe it hurts worse when it's done on your balls.
In fact, it hurts so much that it is usually done under anesthetic. But you know what, I still don't like the idea. I don't even like the idea of the anesthetic needle in my balls.

So, I've got a plan. I'm gonna outsmart them! I'm epilating my balls.

You know epilating? They sell a device called an epilator, usually for ladies to remove fine hairs from their legs and underarms. The Epilady is one well-known model, but there are several others. They have either a spring or spinning discs which grab the hairs and yank them out. Like tweezing, but it does a bunch of hairs rapidly. Also very much like waxing. Does it hurt? Does it *hurt?* Of course it does! It hurts like hell the first time you go over an area. But it's pretty easy after that, as maintenance.

I've epilated my legs, arms and chest. It works great. I just run the epilator over them for 10 minutes or so each week, to catch any re-growth. I'm hopeful that one day the little buggers will take the hint and stop coming back.

So now I am epilating my pubic hairs. I do a little bit every day, just until the tears are streaming down my face. I have to be really careful
to stretch the skin tight, because the epilator will pinch it. I'm making progress. I've gotten almost everything cleared already.

I hope this works. I hope I don't have to do electrolysis of the balls.

(Leans forward as though talking into the camera.)

Yes, Mom, this is the lifestyle I've chosen.

THE BEST BOYFRIEND

JESSE, a young Transgender Man

JESSE stands alone center stage. He's dressed in a three-piece suit, fairly conservative, with a neat haircut and an immaculate shave. As he speaks, he slowly undresses himself, at first as though he's coming home after a date, later because he wants us to see.

(*Smiling.*) She said I was the best boyfriend she'd ever had. No one was ever so sweet to her, she said, so gentle. She said I wasn't like the other guys at all, the ones who forced themselves on her, who never listened to what she had to say. She said I treated her right.

(He takes off his jacket and hangs it neatly on a chair.)

I met her in the park, sort of a classic movie moment. I was sitting on a bench, reading, and she came over. Or rather her dog did. This scruffy little mutt just started sniffing me and licking my hand. So I played with the dog for a minute, until she came looking for him. She smiled, and said he doesn't usually like men, so you must be something special.

(He has unbuttoned his vest during the previous statement and now takes it off and folds it, and places it on top of the jacket.)

I didn't know what to say to that. So I kinda blushed, and patted the dog. And, I don't know what it was, maybe something about that little ball of fluff nosing into my hand, or the way she looked at me when she called me "special," but I asked her for her phone number. She smiled — God, it was beautiful — and asked if I had anything to write with. I didn't.

(He is loosening his tie now, and hangs it neatly over the other clothes when he has taken it off.)

I told her I'd remember anyway. 435-7901. I remembered it, all right. I kept repeating it all the way home. The subway guy asked to see my ticket, and I said 435-7901. A little old lady asked me what time it was: 435-7901. My roommate asked what's for dinner...yep, 435-7901. He said it sounded French.

So I called her, finally. Took me 14 tries, and my roommate still had to practically force me. I'm just shy, ya know?

(He sits down, unties his shoes, and slips them off.)

So we went out to dinner, got to know each other, the whole bit. She was sweet, and gorgeous, and funny...I used to laugh really hard all the time. She liked me, even took me home to meet her parents. They liked me too.

(His socks should be off by now.)

We were really close. Dating. Maybe even in love. She said I was the best boyfriend she'd ever had. And so *(Stands.)* the inevitable happened.

(Undoes belt, unzips fly, pants fall to the floor. He's serious now.)

Sex. She wanted to have sex.

(He steps out of his pants and places them carefully on the rest of the clothes. He's wearing boxer briefs. We see the bulge of his cock underneath.)

So did I, I guess. *(Beat.)* No, I did. Really. I mean, I was in love with her. And she was so hot.

(He's unbuttoning his shirt now. Underneath he wears a white undershirt.)

I just didn't know how to tell her...

(He stands still for a moment in his shirt and underwear.)

So I let it happen. I know I shouldn't have, but everything was so normal. So cheesy, romantic-comedy that I didn't think anything could go wrong.

(He pulls his undershirt over his head. His chest is bound tight with an ace bandage.)

At first she thought I had been in some terrible accident or something.

(He unwinds the bandage, slowly revealing his breasts.)

But no, it was no accident. That's when she stopped talking. She just looked at me. Stared at my chest like she's never seen tits before. I didn't know what to do, so I just kept getting undressed.

(He removes a packy [rubber cock] from his shorts, sets it down.)

I think that's when she started to cry. When I pulled out my dick.

That's when she left. *(Pause.)* Then it got really ugly. You don't need to hear about that. Her father, or the restraining order, or the police.

(He pulls off his shorts and stands naked, looking at the audience.)

Just remember. She said I was the best boyfriend she'd ever had.

(He picks up his clothes, and exits.)

END OF PLAY

ABOUT THE AUTHOR

Tobias K. Davis ("Toby") currently works, lives, and writes in Massachusetts with his beloved partner cmoore and their many pets: Albee the Standard Poodle with the nonstandard haircut, Milton and Chaucer the distinguished tuxedo cats, and Daedalus and Icarus the mischievous caique parrots. He is a transgender activist, playwright, and aspiring young adult novelist. His works have been well received by both the transgender community and the theater community at large. He strives to create works which are entertaining, educational, and accessible.

Davis received his B.A. in Theatre and Italian at Smith College in 2003 and his Master's Degree in Education with a focus on Social Justice at the University of Massachusetts, Amherst, in 2013. He wonders if he will need to get another degree in 10 years to keep up the trend.

He is the author of *Standards of Care*, called "Arguably the best play yet written about female-to-male (FTM) transgender life" by John Townsend of Lavender Magazine, as well as short plays *Jack and Diane*, *Arts and Sciences*, and *Crossing*.

You can visit his website at www.tobiaskdavis.com.

CPSIA information can be obtained
at www.ICGtesting.com
Printed in the USA
LVHW091614260720
661568LV00003B/388

9 780985 535216